The 7 Effective Communication Skills

The 7 Effective Communication Skills

How to be a Better Communicator NOW

Gabriel Angelo

SN & NS

PUBLICATIONS

ISBN 978-1-511-77861-9

Printed in the United States of America

First Edition

THE 7 COMMUNICATION SKILLS

What is Communication?

- 11 -

Skill 1: Effective Verbal Communication

- 17 -

Skill 2: The Importance of Listening

- 23 -

Skill 3: Reading Body Language

- 29 -

Skill 4: Genuine Empathy in Communication

- 35 -

Skill 5: Communicating Confidently

- 41 -

Skill 6: Charisma and Influence for Better Communication

- 56 -

<u>Skill 7: How to Be Cooperative and Handle Difficult People</u>

- 55 -

<u>Summary of Communication</u>

- 62 -

INTRODUCTION

Communication can be considered one of the building blocks of our society. It is what allows people to connect daily through the sharing of knowledge, thoughts, feelings, and wants. Ever since the first grunts shared between primitive men, it is apparent that the process of communication is intertwined into every part of our lives. Without communication, how does the mother know what her baby needs? How does the boss let his employee know what is needed for the project? How does the fast food worker know what you want for lunch? It's all about the communication!

WHAT IS COMMUNICATION?

Communication is the process wherein people share their thoughts or opinions in different ways. It is not true that people can only communicate through words. People can communicate in other ways, e.g., a hand gesture or a simple nod. Communication helps people become understood.

What many do not realize is that communication can extend beyond the active participants within a conversation. This means that even if you are just communicating with one person, there is always a possibility that a third party is hearing what you are saying or is able to decipher any non-verbal signals that you have given. Communication can be done intentionally, but sometimes it is also unintentional.

There are three steps that people undergo when they are communicating. First is the **thought process**, wherein the person thinks about what he or she would like to say to an intended receiver of that thought. Second is the **delivery process**, which is the method used to deliver the thought process to the intended receiver. Possible methods used could include words, actions, or signals. Third is the **receiving process**, where the intended receiver understands the thought process effectively.

When these three processes are successfully accomplished, an effective communication has been completed. However, there are instances when a person's message can get lost in amongst the words and signals. Some of these reasons miscommunication may occur include the following:

- *Language barrier* – There are times when people who have to communicate with each other do not speak the same language. Even with the help of hand signals and other non-verbal communication tactics, language can still play a huge factor in misunderstandings.

- *Misinterpretation* – A person may mean one thing, but the receiver interprets it differently. This usually happens when two people who are communicating with each other are not clearly stating their intent with appropriate word choices and/or actions.

- *Poor listening skills* – Sometimes, no matter how effectively one person tries to communicate with another person, the message is still not received because the intended receiver does not want to listen, is not fully paying attention to the conversation, or is thinking about what he/she wants to say next.

Why is Communication Important?

Many experts have already said that people will not be able to effectively accomplish on their own. This is why they need other people to help them out in one way or another. You cannot ask people to help you without intentionally asking for their help. You need to communicate with them in such a way that they will clearly understand so they will know why you need their help, why you are asking them specifically for help, and how they can help you.

Remember, you are not communicating merely in order to ask for the help of other people. More often than not, we communicate with others to bond with them. This means that we can build better social relationships with people if we can talk with them effectively. Have you ever wondered why, in the dating world, two people do not hit it off? It is because they find they have no foundation upon which to start, much less build, a conversation. They feel they are on two different planets, even when they are at the same location. Two people who have things in common to talk about and can understand each other perfectly can communicate effectively. That is truly important.

When it comes to organizations, communication is also important because there are situations where complex ideas will need to be shared. Without proper communication skills, a person will not be able to find the right words to help people understand what he is trying to say. It is important that a person is sure about his idea and able to state it clearly. He should know what needs to be done and how it can be effective; otherwise, the idea will not be considered by his colleagues.

Effective communication can be helpful in the following situations:

- *Managing departments* – A manager must have effective communication skills because he will be in charge of people who are part of his department. If he is not effective in communicating what he would like to have done, then productivity of the employees will not be high. Tasks will not be finished on time, projects delayed, and output lowered.

- *Businesses* – Effective communication is important in businesses because you always have to speak with other people regarding the different aspects of the business. You will have to communicate with partners and discuss different things that will not be understood correctly if you do not know how to communicate effectively.

- *Raising awareness* – There are different organizations right now that believe in certain causes and they would not be able to ask other people for help without being able to effectively communicate what they would like to say.

Aside from the things mentioned above, there are many other areas in this world that can be improved upon if people would communicate effectively. There are just some people who are not normally good in communicating verbally, so they tend to not speak up.

It is important to remember that, in communicating with people, you may not always have to have perfect grammar. Your communication style may vary based on the situation. What matters is that you know what your current thought is and how you would like to get the message across. If you do not understand what you are trying to say, chances are that people will not understand it either. So, if you know and you truly believe in what you would like to say, you will find ways that are verbal, or even non-verbal, to help people understand.

Communicating effectively may take some work, but making the effort to be understood will pay off in the long run. Here are some skills to help you achieve your goals.

SKILL 1

Do you think that you are a good speaker? Some people are naturally good at it, while others have to work harder in order to be effective. What about you? Do you think people can understand you well through the words that you choose? If your answer is "No", then read on to learn more about being a better speaker.

EFFECTIVE VERBAL COMMUNICATION

Have you ever said something that made people perfectly understand what you want? It has already been said that the main reason that people are able to understand each other well is because they are able to effectively communicate their thoughts with each other. Most of the time, people are able to build relationships with other people through simple conversations.

Verbal communication is important in this day and age. Everyone learns to communicate initially in their native language. You will embrace and master it as you grow older. Even though English is said to be the universal language, it does not mean that everyone needs to know how to speak it. It may be important to know in some places, but in other places, a person's native language is enough.

Not understanding another person's language is obviously a big hindrance when it comes to verbal communication. No matter how many times a person repeats some words, it will mean nothing to you if you don't speak the same language. This is probably the reason why some people resort to using non-verbal communication (discussed below) when they desperately want to be understood.

While the most common method of verbal communication is done face to face, it can also be accomplished over the phone. When speaking over the phone, people will have to rely on their tone and choice of words in order to be understood.

Key Components of Communicating Verbally

- *Language* – People will need to know how to speak a common language in order to be understood. A language barrier can be a hindrance to two people who would like to understand each other.

- *Way of speaking* – Sometimes, even though the language is not understood, the way a person says some words will still give people an idea about what the other person is talking about. It can be a big help if a person knows the right way to speak.

- *Sound* – You can tell if a person is angry or happy from the way a person intonates each word. This is also connected to the facial expressions that people use in order to convey their message.

There are some people who are naturally good at communicating with other people. They simply need to say a few words and people will automatically understand them. But, if you are not the type of person who is requested to make speeches or has a difficult time speaking with others, then you probably need to do a few things in order to improve your conversation skills.

Improving Your Conversation Skills

You can always improve your conversation skills by following these simple steps:

1. Make sure that you speak your words clearly and audibly. Have you ever wanted someone to repeat what they have said because their voice seems muffled or you did not hear some of

the words? You will only be able to communicate and converse effectively with other people if you speak each word clearly.

2. Directly related to the first tip is the habit of speaking slowly. Speaking fast can cause you to mispronounce words or jumble your words together, making it difficult for others to understand you. Take the time to clearly state your words.

3. Be observant towards the person to whom you are talking. If you want to start a conversation, you may want to pick out something unique about the person and start from there. Remember, noting little details will help people realize that you are interested in having a conversation with them.

4. Know the right words to say. You cannot be offensive or say things that may sound harsh, especially if it is your first time to speak with that person. You have to know what topics are safe for initial conversations and save more complex topics for when a stronger relationship exists.

5. Give compliments. When said at the right time, a compliment can make people feel at ease as the conversation progresses.

Once you apply these things to the way you speak with other people, you will be less worried about saying the wrong thing, even if you are talking to a person of authority or someone you would like to impress.

Etiquette in Verbal Communication

One of the things that you should realize is that etiquette is important when it comes to speaking with other people, especially when you are speaking with people of authority. When you are able to exhibit courtesy and manners during a conversation, it will be easier for you to climb higher on the corporate ladder.

Remember, the things you say to other people have to make sense. In a business setting, you need to have the right ideas that will help the company succeed. If you keep on saying things that have already been said or things that are not relevant to the situation at hand, then it is likely that your bosses will overlook you. Then, when you do have the million-dollar idea, you will not be taken seriously because they will think that it's just one of your senseless talks.

Listening to what others have to say during a business discussion is also important. In the corporate world, everything is interconnected. You need to have knowledge of the functions of the other departments so that you can understand the comments they make about a particular project to see if your idea is cohesive and can be used on the project. Listening will give you a clue about the department's functions and then you will know if your idea needs to be tweaked to be a viable option.

With the right verbal skills, it will be so much easier to be noticed and be successful.

SKILL 2

Have you ever watched as someone made a situation much worse because they simply kept talking and wouldn't listen? There are instances when talking can be the worst thing that someone can do. If you think that communication is only about speaking, then you are mistaken. You also have to learn how to listen well in order to be a good communicator. Being attentive will create a positive impression when you are talking with other people.

THE IMPORTANCE OF LISTENING

One of the first things that people think about when they hear the word communication is the act of speaking. While verbal communication is important, you also have to know how to listen so you can understand what the other person is saying. We often assume that, once something has been said, it has already been understood by people involved in the conversation. This is not true. There are times when people need to hear things more than once because they have not listened as closely as they should have the first time around.

Unfortunately, many people do not even attempt to listen to other people. Once they have already decided that they know what is right for them, they do not bother trying to see another point of view. This can be a huge problem because, if people will not listen to each other, communication will become fruitless. Remember, communication is only effective when a person speaks his thoughts and the listener truly listens and processes the thoughts conveyed.

You may be surprised by the fact that many people do not know how to listen. Yet, it is actually considered to be quite normal. This is because most people have not been taught how to listen. Even if they have, they choose to actively not listen because they believe that they already know everything. It has been said that people learn when they listen. So, if we do not listen, we will not learn.

Improving Your Listening Skills

Here are some tips to follow so that you can have better listening skills:

1. Make sure that you are not distracted. Sometimes, people feel that they cannot listen because there are so many external distractions, such as noises that may be keeping you from listening to the speaker. There are also instances when the

distractions are internal. This means that you are thinking intently about something and you cannot listen to what is being said because your thoughts are preoccupied with another topic.

2. You do not know the different levels of listening. You may be surprised to know that there are different levels of listening. You have to concentrate more when instructions are being conveyed to you as compared to listening to the local news at night. Learning these levels will allow you to focus on the things that need your attention.

- *Discriminative listening* – Distinguishing between sounds—tone, rate of speech, pitch—to identify a message when the spoken word is not clearly understood.

- *Comprehensive listening* – Learning and understanding through the actual spoken words and their meanings, as well as the sounds of how they're spoken.

- *Critical listening* – Evaluating and judging to form your own conclusion or criticism to respond back.

- *Appreciative listening* – Enjoying the sounds of a pleasurable activity, such as listening to your favorite music or going to a movie.

- *Empathetic listening* – Connecting and relating to people by putting yourself in their shoes and really understanding them to create a favorable bond.

3. Realize the important points. Whenever people are speaking verbally, there are key words used to highlight the main points. These may be words indicating a list (first, second, third) or the speaker may even say "Remember this!" to emphasize a point. Once you have been able to identify the important points, you will be able to put them together to see the overall theme that is being communicated.

4. Do not interrupt. This is probably one of the things that annoys people the most. When people feel that they have something important that they would like to share, they want you to listen as intently as possible. Interrupting will only show that you are not interested in what they have to say and that you would rather listen to your own thoughts and beliefs instead.

5. Stay focused on what is being said. Letting your mind wander will distract you and cause you to be lost in the conversation because you will have no idea as to what was just said. No matter how uninteresting the topic is to you, you have to make sure that you do your best to listen attentively because, most of the time, people just need to be heard.

Listening During Daily Conversations

When you are listening to a friend of yours or a family member talk about a problem, you want to empathize with him or her as much as possible. Empathizing will show the person that you care and are interesting in helping to somehow ease the burden. However, this could be an instance of him or her just wanting to be heard and not necessarily receive advice. They just want to say their piece so that it will get out of their system. If your advice is not being asked, do not offer any. The moment that the person asks for your advice though, give your honest opinion about how you view the situation. Your response should include specific references regarding the problem, which will show that you have been listening. Not listening while your friend or family member is talking may hurt his or her feelings, so make sure that you give your full attention to the person during the conversation.

Listening During Talks/Meetings/In Class

It can be a bit harder to listen when you are with a large group of people and there is only one speaker. You need to remember that it is even harder for the speaker to explain what he or she would like to say to a group of people who may look like they are paying attention, but are not really listening. This is probably the challenge of most professors in any college. The students know that they need to listen in order to take notes and make good grades, but because of different reasons, they lose their attention and they let their minds wander a bit. That has got to be frustrating for the professor!

In other instances, some people may choose not to listen based on the speaker's looks. You should not judge a person by the way he or she dresses or the way he or she carries himself/herself. Every person has unique thoughts and listening to and attempting to understand those thoughts might help you become a better person in the long run.

Finally, remember that listening to someone does not mean committing to memory each word that the person is saying. Rather, it is understanding the broader context of the message that the person is trying to convey.

SKILL 3

Have you ever wondered why there are some people who can easily read body language? Some people are naturally good at it, but most people have to study body language in order to better understand it and interpret its meaning. This section will help you do just that.

READING BODY LANGUAGE

Crossing your arms in front of your chest while you are talking to someone, tilting your head to the side as someone is explaining a concept to you—these are examples of body language that most people do often, even if they are not aware of it. While there are some who have made interpreting body language a professional choice, most people are simply clueless. While they know that they may be incorporating body language into their own messages, they are unable to pick up on these clues when other people do it as well.

Many experts have said that body language comprises a huge part of non-verbal communication. This means that, aside from other non-verbal signs that people use, it is body language that is most widely used by people all over the world.

How Can You Decipher Body Language?

You cannot understand body language by trying to memorize each different action and then connecting it with a specific meaning. There are always differences in situations or events that may change the meaning of an action. However, there are some signals that you can look for in order to make it easier for you to read someone's body language. Here are some of the most common signals:

- *Facial expressions* – Many people use facial expressions in order to convey what they are trying to say or feel. There are numerous emotions that people can show through their facial expressions—happy, sad, angry, frustrated. However, there are people who are good at masking their emotions so their real feelings will not show. But, most people are not able to conceal their feelings and it typically shows on their face.

- *Eyes* – Ever wonder why poker players wear sunglasses inside while at the table? They do this so they can keep their eyes hidden to conceal any "tells" they may inadvertently expose during the hand. While there are some things that the face can hide, the eyes will often reveal them. When someone is really interested in a conversation, there is a light in the eyes, as opposed to a glazed-over look that implies that he or she is not interested. The eyes can also expose a nervous nature or an intent to hide something, as seen when a person may constantly blink or dart their eyes around to avoid eye contact with another person.

- *People's gestures* – Some people naturally make a lot of hand movements when they talk; others do not. There are times when you will be able to tell if the person is nervous or is hiding something by what they do with their hands. Are they wringing their hands or rubbing them in a nervous way? This could be an indicator that something is wrong.

- *Posture* – Some studies state that a person's posture can say a lot about how attentive he or she is during a conversation. Talking to someone who is slumped down in a chair might show that he or she is not engaged in the conversation as opposed to someone who is sitting upright and seems to be paying full attention. But, do not always discount someone because of this as there are some people who simply have bad posture.

- *Mouth* – Aside from the eyes, the mouth can also convey what a person is currently feeling without speaking. There are some things that people do with their mouths when they are not feeling confident or when they are feeling a bit anxious. You may notice a tightening around the lips that could indicate anger. Or, a person might bite their lip, showing nervousness.

These are just a few of the examples of body language that people use every day. There are many other examples and interpretations that have not been included above that can still help you determine what the other person is trying to convey. The important thing to remember about body language is that it is typically an unconscious action and people are not able to control it. This is when their true feelings become evident. So, the more you understand about body language, the more you will be able to decipher the current emotions of the person involved in the conversation with you.

Importance of Non-Verbal Communication

Time and time again, we have said that communication is important so that people will understand each other perfectly. But, did you realize that people communicate non-verbally rather than verbally most of the time?

Haven't you ever had that moment when you know that you have to say something, but you do not believe what you are saying? More often than not, people have to say something that they do not really mean in order to get out of an unpleasant situation or to ease the burden of someone else. Through non-verbal gestures and movements, you will still be able to get your point across.

Here are some examples of moments when people use non-verbal communication:

1. To strengthen those words being said. A person who is being truthful in the verbal words that he is saying might want to strengthen the honesty of the words by making sure that the non-verbal and verbal ways of communication are being portrayed in a synchronized manner. An example of this would be to make sure that eye contact is being made to emphasize the truthfulness of a statement.

2. To accent or make words stronger. If you would like to prove a point, you may do some gestures that will support the things that you have just said. Just be careful that your gestures do not come across as too aggressive to the other person.

3. To make people realize things or to convey messages without having to say a word. For those who are not too good with words, they may choose to communicate non-verbally to avoid saying the wrong thing. This is done in the hopes that the message will be better understood by the other person (or persons) involved in the conversation.

What Should You Believe More?

There are times when people become confused about which communication method they should believe—the person's words (verbal) or the person's actions (non-verbal). Most of the time, people say what is right or what they think is correct in a particular situation. But, if the person is not able to follow through with subsequent actions, the person probably did not mean what was said originally. Non-verbal communication is more believable because it is unconscious and hard to control. Basically, it exposes our true feelings to the world, even if we do not mean it to.

SKILL 4

There are times when you cannot help but sympathize when you hear the stories of other people. There are also times you feel empowered when you hear good speakers share success stories. Wouldn't you want to be that speaker that people respect? Wouldn't you want to have the ability to speak your mind and relate to people from all walks of life? You can always start by being empathic, which you can learn more about in this section.

GENUINE EMPATHY IN COMMUNICATION

Have you ever had that moment when you are watching something dramatic on TV and, before you know it, a tear slides down your cheek? You are feeling emotions because you can understand the character's situation and care about what is going to happen. When this occurs, you are practicing empathy for the person and the situation that you see on screen.

Empathy is said to be something that is important in communication. There are times when people misunderstand what empathy is because it is more of an emotion, not a cold, hard fact.

So, why is empathy important in communication? It is simple—people are able to better communicate with others if their empathy level is high because that means that they have the ability to put themselves in the other person's shoes and understand the other person's situation better.

How to Be Empathic

Even if empathy is very important in communication, there are some who are not able to use it well because they do not have effective communication skills. You would need to know how to communicate both verbally and non-verbally in order to understand others and be understood in return. You might be a bit confused as to why you would need good communication skills in order to be empathic, but it is not about the speaking part, but how you listen.

You have to have the ability to listen closely so that you will understand the other person's situation. When you listen, you are lending an ear to the person. You are putting yourself in his or her shoes and through that, plus an active imagination, you are able to understand what the person is going through.

Everybody sees the world differently. No matter how close you are to a person, it does not mean that you see things 100% the same way. Even if you go through the same situations, you will remember some details better than others, while the other person may have been focusing on completely different details and will recall them better. This is because we are all different and rate the importance of things in our lives differently. Because of this, being able to understand another person's point of view or feel for them as they go through a complex personal situation is an important communication skill.

How to Get People to Like You

When people are able to show empathy towards others, there is a stronger understanding between them because they are showing concern for each other. But before someone can feel empathy for you, they must first like you. How do you make people like you? If everybody knew the answer to this question, the world would be a much better place. Here are some tips to help create a likable personality:

- *Smile* – When people are smiling, they look more approachable. A lot of people are shy and are not able to randomly approach other people. If you keep a genuine smile on your face, it will draw people towards you and, of course, like you better.

- *Say "Thank You" more often* – When you say thank you, it makes people feel good because their assistance, no matter how small it may have been, was acknowledged and appreciated. Saying thank you makes it seem like you are overflowing with good things to say about other people. That will make people want to be by your side more.

- *Look strong and peaceful at the same time* – How is this possible when there are so many things happening around us? In this world, there is a lot of chaos and problems that people encounter every single day. If you keep your cool and look like you are confident in the midst of the storm, then people would want to be just like you. This may be a hard thing to do, but practice makes perfect.

- *Talk about positive things* – If you are speaking with someone for the first time, it may be best to keep the conversation light. Focus on easy topics that will not require you to have diverse opinions. If you find yourself in a discussion that has started to get heated because of some strong opinions being shared, try to steer things back to some less-complicated topics.

- *Be genuine* – This is probably the most important thing. In this world right now, we do not want to be with people who do not truly like us. If you are honest about how you feel and you are naturally genuine, more and more people will like you. This also applies to doing good things for other people. However, if you want to do good things for others, you need to be sure you are doing it because you want to and not because you are seeking a reward or asking for something in return.

These are just a few pointers on how to get people to like you. Take some time to learn about yourself—what are your positive traits? What good deeds have you done? When you know these things about yourself, you will be able to share them in an open and honest way with others and create opportunities for new relationships.

The Most Important Thing

While there are several important things when it comes to communication, the most important thing is actually being sincere.

This can be applied to almost everything that we do. When we talk, we have to be sincere. If we are not sincere, then people will not want to listen to us.

When we are sincere in listening to other people, they will feel it. They will become more active in talking about themselves because they know that we are genuinely interested in listening to them. They will tend to feel more confident about the things that they would like to say. It will also make them more honest about what they feel because they trust you more to speak truthfully.

Have you ever wondered why it is that, even in silence, there is a sense of comfort when you are with a person? It is because there is a level of shared honesty and sincerity. You do not have to communicate verbally to understand each other well.

Empathy, sincerity, and being generally liked will help you greatly in sharing your messages. In the long run, they may matter more than being able to speak well verbally.

SKILL 5

One of the things that can hinder people from being able to say what they want to say is a lack of confidence in themselves. Most people feel that when they say something, others will automatically judge them. If you are confident in yourself and what you are saying, it will be evident to the others involved in the conversation and they will be more open to hearing what you have to say.

COMMUNICATING CONFIDENTLY

Many people have good ideas, but they are often not heard because they are not confident enough to voice their opinion. Some people are born naturally confident and have a charisma about them which enables them to talk to just about anyone. Then, there are those who struggle with their words, causing them to be more of a passive participant in the conversation, allowing others to steer the conversation and shine.

When a shy person is finally given the opportunity to speak to a group, several things can happen. He might simply freeze and forget what he was going to say. Or, he may get the words out, but tend to sound robotic and not be able to present a convincing statement. A lack of confidence will truly kill any idea, no matter how brilliant the idea is. Presentation matters!

How to Become Confident

Confidence cannot be learned overnight. You might struggle through the process of trying to build your confidence, but once you have it, you begin to realize that you have been missing something great all along—a belief in yourself. To start building your confidence, follow these tips:

- *Practice* – When you are alone at night, practice how you will stand, smile, and greet people as they approach you. Do not overdo it and become too routine at it, though, as it may come off looking like you are forcing your actions instead of them being natural.

- *Stand straight and tall* – You can change the way you feel by adopting a confident stance and/or keeping a positive expression on your face. Having your shoulders straight and back projects an image of confidence and of an attitude that you can accomplish anything. By the same token, having slouched shoulders and a frown will cause people to feel that you are incapable of handling even the simplest task.

- *Self-competence* – Being confident is more than attitude. If you want to sound like you know what you are talking about, then know what you are talking about. Take time to study on related topics before meetings or presentations so that your comments come across as thoughtful and relevant. As you continue to do this, your knowledge of general things will increase and so will your confidence in making conversation with others, whether in the boardroom or the corner bar.

How Being Confident Can Help You

At this point, it may not yet be clear to you as to why you need to become confident in your communication skills. Being confident does not mean being obnoxious or dominating all of the conversation when with other people. Generally, confident people are assertive in a positive manner and they can balance speaking in a group with listening to the group. As your new confidence allows you to build more relationships with other people, you will also start to enjoy the following benefits:

1. Being confident can help you get what you want out of life. We all have certain hopes and dreams that we would like to see accomplished during our lives. But, the road to getting these things is not always easy. Being confident can help you handle the ups and downs on that road better because you will be able to push your way forward through the valleys to the top of the hill each time with a confident nature. Remember, when you are confident, your faith in yourself will have you reaching all the goals that you have set for yourself.

2. When you are confident, you are more comfortable with your beliefs and in taking action based on those beliefs. You will be able to speak more firmly when asked for an opinion because you know who you are. That may sound silly, but it's true. When others second-guess themselves and go back and forth over every decision, it can make them seem weaker. Others will be less inclined to look to that person for leadership. They will follow the person with a decisive nature that can clearly communicate his decisions.

3. Being confident generally makes you happy. You may not realize this in the beginning, but when you feel confident about yourself and what you do, you tend to look at the world in a more positive light. You see the good things more than the bad

and you have the tendency to count your blessings more, which of course is a good thing.

Being Positive

Another important thing in communication is being positive. Whenever people are positive, they tend to attract more people towards them. People want to associate themselves with people who radiate positivity, because honestly, they would like to feel the same way.

It may seem easy to say that you are going to start being positive, and it is easy to say that. The hard part is to accept that you are going to have to remove all the negative things that are impacting your life. If you would like to be a positive person, there are certain things that you can do, such as the following:

Forget All Negative Thoughts

If you keep on focusing on the things that you have failed at in life, you will not be able to move on to being a more positive person. Every situation, whether it is a good or a bad one, will have a positive and negative side to it. The key is to acknowledge both sides, but only take the positive effects of the situation away with you. Eventually, you will see that this will change you for the better.

Avoid Influences That Are Negative

Remember the "Debbie Downer" character from *Saturday Night Live*? She is the person who can find the negative side of any situation and then talk about it constantly, generally lowering the mood of any get-together. Even if you can remove all of the negative thoughts from your own head, it would be hard to keep them out if your circle of friends consists of a lot of "Debbie Downers". Instead, surround yourself with happy people and you will find that your own outlook on life will improve.

Avoid Worrying

Focusing on negative thoughts and stories creates a by-product—worry. Often, people worry about things that they simply cannot control, such as war, crime, or health issues. While these are things that deserve thoughtful consideration, they should not preoccupy you to the point that you feel weighted down by the problems of the world. The key is to change your approach and take charge of the situation. Worried about crime? Take steps to secure your home and belongings. Worried about your health? Eat healthy, exercise, and visit your doctor regularly. Knowing that you have taken steps to manage the things that can worry you will create a confidence in you that can translate to taking charge in business situations too.

Have a "Happy Thought"

Maybe your "happy thought" is a special vacation. Maybe it is a person. It could even be your puppy. The point is that, when you think of it, you mind switches to a more positive channel. So, every time you feel in the midst of a bout of loneliness or start to have a worry circle your mind, envision your "happy thought" over and over. It is likely that your body will start to recognize it as a positive reinforcement and will block the negativity.

Remember, being confident, being positive, and being assertive in the things that you believe in will help you when you are communicating with other people.

SKILL 6

It is important to be able to keep the attention of those to whom you are speaking. If you appear to be shy, hesitant, or unknowledgeable, then you will lose your audience. It is essential that you develop the ability to share your message in a way that will ensure that people will know what points you are trying to make. But, you do not just want them to know what those points are, you want them to embrace those points and join you on your team. That may take some charisma and persuasion skills.

CHARISMA AND INFLUENCE FOR BETTER COMMUNICATION

Have you ever had that moment when you badly need to take a leave from work, but you weren't able to convince your boss to approve it? This probably means that you lack some persuasion skills (or maybe you just have too many things to do in the office). Gaining the skill of persuasion is like learning that you have the ability to use The Force from Star Wars. You can use it for good or evil. If you use it for the benefit of your work team, as when you persuade a client to sign a deal with your company, then it can be a good thing. But, if you use it to take advantage of others, e.g. convincing someone to take your shift when they really do not have the time, then obviously you are abusing your powers.

Persuasion in communication is important because you want to have the person (or group) that you are speaking to not only see your point of view, but understand why that view is the optimal position. If you are normally a submissive person, it may be a bit hard for you to be persuasive. Try incorporating the following tips:

- *Appear confident* – When people see you as someone with confidence, they will assume that you have sensible things to say. Even though you may not be there yet in terms of knowing the right things to say, standing straight and looking people in the eyes will go a long way towards projecting a confident nature.

- *Make your voice stable and enthusiastic* – One of the things that can put off people is when you continuously make unnecessary pauses when talking. An uneven tone or muttered words can also distract people from whatever point you are trying to make. Remember, how your voice sounds will have an effect on the people listening to you. If necessary, take a calming breath before beginning any speeches or count to 10 to try to calm any jittery nerves.

- *Know the answers to the questions that will be asked* – When you are trying to persuade others to agree with your point of view on a certain topic, there will be some questions coming your way. You should know the answer to these questions so that people will realize that you have taken the time to research the points in your argument, showing your commitment to and knowledge about the topic.

- *Be calm* – Do not be one of those people who lose their cool during a conversation because others will not agree with them. When others present opposing views, do not complain or become upset just because the conversation is not going your way. It is important to listen to others' points and then calmly re-state your position. Remaining calm will give the impression of control, which is important when trying to persuade others to believe in your cause or idea.

- *Know your audience* – Know who you will be talking to before you go into a meeting or gathering. Is the crowd a conservative crowd or a liberal one? Is it a room full of stay-at-home moms or young professionals? When you know the demographics of the audience, you can better tailor your comments specifically for them. This again will show that you have put some research into your presentation and cause others to generally have an impression of you as an organized and prepared person.

Being Charismatic and Influential

When a person is charismatic, it means that they have a way of interacting with others that can create a sense of loyalty or special feeling towards the person. How one speaks is an important tool of a charismatic person. The tone used and the connections created through words can cause listeners to view the speaker in an idolized way, which in turn makes them more inclined to agree with speaker's views.

One of the easiest ways to connect to an audience is to tell stories that you know will help catch their attention. Going back to the example above regarding "Know your audience", let's look at how you would connect with the two different groups—stay-at home moms and young professionals—on the subject of organization. For moms, you might tell a story of the chaos that can happen when you are trying to get the kids out the door for school and you are fumbling for their homework, lunches, etc. For the young professionals, it may be a story about a messy office and how you can't find the notes you need for a project deadline. The details may be different, but the point is the same—being organized can help you accomplish things more efficiently. Once you have that connection with them on a personal level, then anything that you want to sell or promote to them will be easier because they know that you "understand" them.

It is also important to make sure that you state your views with conviction. Your audience will be able to tell if you truly believe what you are saying based on your tone and your energy level. If you feel strongly about something, you are pumped up and excited to share it with others. If your attitude is so-so about your presentation, then that will come across as you not believing in the product or idea yourself. If you do not believe in it, why should they?

Have you ever wondered why it seems it is always the same people endorsing products on television or in print ads? It is because those people are influential and have a huge following, which translates into more sales. Remember the segment, "Oprah's Favorite Things" on her TV show? How many people went out and bought the items highlighted on the show just because they were on

Oprah's list? Thousands and thousands! That's what can happen when you have influence.

When it comes to communication, though, being influential does not mean that people have to purchase your products. Rather, it means that you hope they will listen to what you have to say and agree with you.

So how can you become influential? Here are a few qualities to work on to increase your influential factor:

1. *Have interpersonal skills* – You have to be the type of person who can approach almost anyone and be able to make that person feel good. Influential people are not afraid of being rejected because their social skills will allow them to move on from a negative situation with minimum impact upon themselves. While you may think that this is only applicable to face-to-face communications, it is possible for influential people to change the tone of a discussion on social media as well.

2. *Be passionate* – If you personally do not have passion for the things that you are discussing with other people, it will show. You cannot share something that you do not have. To have a

higher percentage of success, you should focus your skills on promoting things that you care about because those are the topics that you will be able to use to create a connection with others.

Remember, being charismatic and persuasive must go hand in hand. It is difficult to be persuasive if you do not have a charismatic nature because people will just feel like you are trying to sell them something. On the other hand, just being charismatic is not enough either. You have to be able to use your charisma when making your points in order to persuade others to adopt your viewpoints.

SKILL 7

There are over 7 billion on this planet. The odds of having only people in your life that agree with you constantly are so small that they probably can't be calculated. So, learning how to cooperate with others and deal with difficult people are important skills to master.

HOW TO BE COOPERATIVE AND HANDLE DIFFICULT PEOPLE

Imagine that the boss has put together a team to work on a new project and has made you the project leader. There are colleagues from other departments that you did not even know existed that are now working with you. You have some definite ideas that you think will work well for the project and you want to make sure that your views are heard. But, you also know that you have to be open to listening to others' opinions and create a positive working environment. How can you accomplish this so that your goals and deadlines are met?

This is a common scenario played out in offices throughout the business world. On this team, you may have some people who find it hard to cooperate because they have a more domineering personality and are used to being the one in charge. Others may be more reserved and not participate as much as you would like; basically, they are not carrying their weight for the team because their past history has caused them to believe that their opinions have no value. Then, there are those who have the ability to be leaders themselves, but also know how to be a follower.

Being Cooperative

With all these personalities on a team, being cooperative can make things run a lot smoother. However, if you are not the cooperative type, you should practice the following tips to help promote harmony within your group:

- *Listen* – This is actually one of the hardest things for some people to do because they simply do not want to listen to other people. It is also one of the easiest ways to show others that you are non-cooperative. If you cannot listen to another's point of view, then it shows that you do not have the ability to be flexible and have a "It's my way or the highway" kind of mentality. Either way, it will not win you friends. Leading a task does not mean that you have to do everything on your own. Your other group members are there to help you by carrying out assigned tasks.

- *Participate* – You cannot let your group have healthy discussions without you saying your piece. There are those who do not actively participate in group discussions. They are either not interested in being there or are timid about sharing ideas during a brainstorming session. To be a cooperative member of the group, be alert and involved in the discussions. If you are not ready yet to share ideas, volunteer to take notes. As you participate more, your confidence will grow and you will soon feel comfortable enough to comment on ideas and make relevant points.

- *Encourage* – Offering encouragement is an important part of a cooperative group effort. Remember, people who work in groups are normally pressured to finish something on time. You can be extremely helpful to the group if you lift up their spirits from time to time. It will boost their work and, at the same time, their performance.

- *Have good relationships* – It is important to have positive office relationships. If people are not on speaking terms, then there will obviously be a problem when a team is working together on a project. Focus on building effective working relationships. You do not have to share a drink with them during happy hour every Friday, but you do need to find a way to communicate in a positive way so that the office is not filled with tension. Keep conversations related to work and away from any personal topics. By doing this, you will be able to stay focused on the specifics of the project and not on your differences.

- *Ask relevant questions* – It is advisable to ask questions—relevant questions—in order to make fewer mistakes. If something seems unclear to you, then it's possible that someone else within the group may also not fully understand what was just said. Better to take a few minutes to make sure that everyone is on the same page than to have half the group doing one thing and the other half doing something completely different because a point was misunderstood.

Dealing with Difficult People

Now, you've learned how to be cooperative. But, there will still be people who will challenge you and be very hard to deal with in certain situations. Aside from the fact that they will probably lack communication skills when it comes to speaking with other people, they will also tend to be a bit rude and dismissive of others' ideas. While some people may genuinely be difficult due to their personalities, more often than not, others are difficult simply because they are being caught at the wrong time. They may be dealing with a personal matter that is causing them to act differently than their normal behavior.

So, how can you deal with a difficult person? Admittedly, it can be a bit hard. There will be moments when you just want to give up and not look back as you try to get as far away as possible from them. But, it does not have to end that way. There are things that you can do in order to deal with difficult people and maybe, just maybe, create harmony.

Remember that there will always be people who will be a challenge.

Instead of trying to change the people that you meet, it will be better if you just change how you react every time the person makes your situation harder. Instead of lashing out, it might be best to practice your empathic skills to try to understand the situation from their point of view. Having someone try to see their point of view might be enough to jar them into different, more pleasant, behavior. Remember that people who make your life difficult have feelings and emotions too. Changing the way you deal with them may change their mindset towards you.

It always takes two to make a conflict.

If you think that it is only the other person who is creating conflict in your life, try to remember what your behavior has been in the past towards that person. Have you noticed that you seem to have a lot of people in your life that seem to make it miserable? Perhaps it is not them who need to change, but YOU.

Just breathe.

At those moments when you feel that you cannot deal anymore and you want to break down and cry because of the tense situations around you, just let it out and breathe. If you need to cry, then do so. When your emotions are high, you might do things that you will only regret later on. So, count to 10 to allow yourself time to compose yourself and then come back to the situation.

People will have differences that possibly cannot be changed. But, if we have good communication skills, it will be a breeze to have friends and eventually have a good relationship with the people we have to deal with in both our work and personal lives.

OVERVIEW

From verbal communication to non-verbal communication, everything has to be intentional and effective in order for your message to be understood. This summarizes those things that you should have in your skill set in order to have better conversations with people you meet, and, ultimately, build better relationships in both your personal and professional life.

SUMMARY OF COMMUNICATION

Imagine a world without communication. How would people accomplish anything, whether individually or as part of a team? The simple answer is that nothing would be accomplished. Each person would be in a world of his own, cut off from others because there is no way for feelings, thoughts, or ideas to be shared, or even a way to ask for help.

Communication is a complex matter that has a lot of facets, but if people understand them, they will be better able to effectively share their intended message. Let's do a final review of the things we have learned:

- *What communication skills can do for you.* Effective communication skills can help you achieve the best that you want in your life. Using clear language and corresponding non-verbal signals will help you state your objectives in a manner that will present you in the best light. People will have a better impression of you and come to think of you as a person who has ideas and can make things happen.

- *The importance of verbal communication.* We have all listened to someone and thought, "What are you saying?" Remember, language can be a barrier to effective communication. There are over 6,000 spoken languages in the world today. If you are not communicating with someone in a common language, then it will be difficult to build relationships. Know your local language so that you can use the right words at the right time. And, if you work or travel internationally, then you need to either learn those necessary languages or make sure you have an interpreter knowledgeable in both languages. Speak slowly so that your words can be better understood. Finally, tone is important in expressing the emotions of your words. Make sure they match to better get your point across.

- *How effective listening can also be communication.* Being the listener in a conversation is just as important as being the speaker. Actually, it's impossible to have one without the other. Listening to others will help you understand their situations and it makes the other person feel that their comments have value. This is a vital component of establishing strong relationships, which are necessary in the business and personal situations.

- *Non-verbal communication and how it can affect you.* Hopefully, through reading this article, you have seen how your non-verbal communication, i.e., body language, can betray your honest feelings about a situation, even if you are saying something different. Things such as your eyes, posture, hand gestures, and mouth can unconsciously betray you to the other participants in a conversation. While some can control these movements, many cannot. It can cause people to feel that you are being dishonest with them and affect any decisions they may have to make regarding entering into a personal or business relationship with you.

- *Being empathic.* Empathy is a trait that would benefit most people in this world. Everyone deals with situations differently and being empathetic will allow you to see the situation from their point of view. This compassion and sincerity will be appreciated by those around you, leading to stronger relationships further down the road.

- *Confidence in communication.* Confidence in communication occurs when you are speaking about things for which you have a passion for or in which you are very knowledgeable. It can be seen in your stance and heard in your voice and people will respond to the honest nature of your approach. However, if you are not confident in your topics, then it will show through your stuttered speech, bad posture, and lack of eye contact. This can lead people to feel a level of unease about you and doubt your ability to lead in various situations. Until you can build your level of confidence, practice any speeches or presentations ahead of time so that you are comfortable in presenting the information to groups. Keep your posture straight and tall during conversations.

- *How to be persuasive and influential.* Let's face it—some people are more influential than others. They seem to be able to achieve the things that they want done through partnerships with others. This requires you to have good relationships with your peers, including being well-liked and respected by them. When you have interactions based on respect and trust, you will not have to constantly struggle with others to get things done. Your effective communication skills will allow you to persuade them to work together for the common goal.

- *Being cooperative.* Your business and personal life is full of times when you will have to work with others to get things accomplished in an effective manner. A domineering attitude will not make this happen; neither will a submissive one. The keys to working in groups is to listen to the others in the group, participate in key discussions, encourage the team to continuously move towards accomplishing the objective, and ask relevant questions to make sure the team is working with one goal in mind.

Remember, when it comes to communication, there is a doer (a speaker or a person exhibiting non-verbal communication) and a receiver. When both parties are using good communication skills, such as the ones outlined here, then the message will be effectively conveyed and understood. After all, that is the ultimate goal of communication—to be heard and understood.

The 7 Effective Communication Skills.

Gabriel Angelo. Copyright © SN & NS Publications, All Rights Reserved.

Made in the USA
Middletown, DE
27 August 2018